What's Inside the Book?

KU-464-633

What Is a Family?

Who Takes Care of Me?

big sister

little brother

Brothers and Sisters

twins

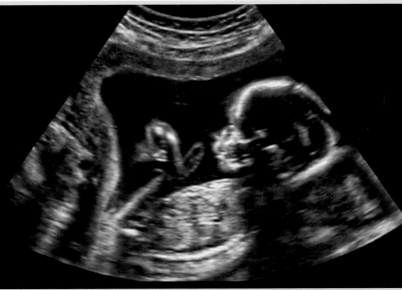

A New Baby

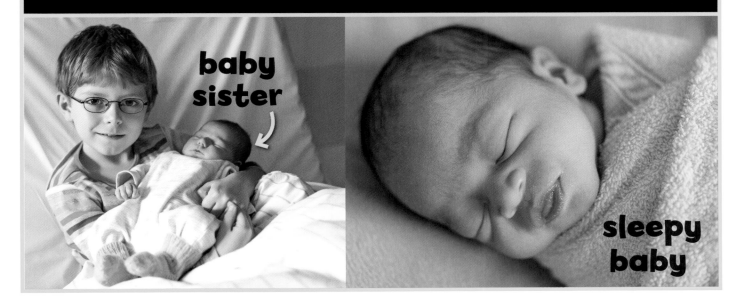

baby
sister

sleepy
baby

mummy

daughter

daddy

son

hungry babies

kiss

11

Our Families

Who is in my family?

grandfather

grandson

granddaughter

grandmother

niece **auntie**

uncle

nephew

cousins

13

cat

dog

Our Pets

rabbit

fish

guinea pig

goat

puppies

hamster

kittens

Where Do Families Live?

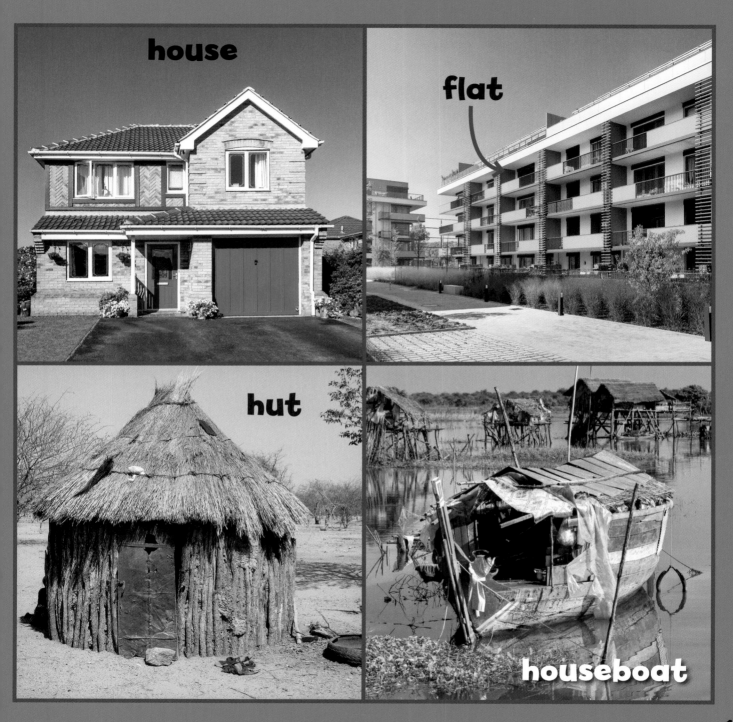

house

flat

hut

houseboat

Helping at Home

collecting firewood

gardening

washing up

cooking

washing the car

breakfast

Let's Eat!

soup

pizza

lunch

picnic

barbecue

Who did you eat with today?

dinner

strawberries

playing

sharing

Things We Do

laughing

hugging

walking

riding a bike

shopping

camping

friends

People in Our World

neighbour

childminder

teacher

lollipop man

postwoman

birthday

Halloween

Celebrations

Christmas

Diwali

Ramadan

iftar

Chinese New Year

happy

Family Feelings

sad

excited

safe

angry

silly

How does my family make me feel?

loved

Tips and Ideas

Look ✓ Read ✓ Talk ✓ Discover ✓ Learn ✓

This book is designed to help you and your child get the best learning experience possible. We suggest that you make yourselves comfortable within a quiet environment and allow your child to hold the book and turn the pages. When you and your child are reading the book, pause to allow your child to *read* a word or ask questions about the pictures and words.

Pages 4-7: As young children experience the world outside their home and start to make friends at school, they may notice that not every family has the same structure. The photographs on these pages help to celebrate that there are many different kinds of families.

When talking with your child about families, explain that a family may have a mummy and a daddy. It might have a mummy and no daddy, or a daddy and no mummy. Some families have two mummies or two daddies, or no mummies and daddies. Some families have two parents that live separately.

Many children live in a blended family with a biological parent and another parent figure. This family may include children that the parent couple have had together and children from previous relationships.

A family may also include parents and one or more adopted children.

Some children live with their grandparents or with aunts and uncles. Others live with foster parents or other guardians.

Explain to your child that every family is unique and any combination of people can make a family. What's most important is that the members of a family love each other and take care of each other.

Talk to your child about who is in THEIR family, who takes care of THEM and who lives in THEIR home.

Pages 10-11: The photographs on these pages can be used to help explain the arrival of a new baby to a family. On page 10, the woman in the striped top is pregnant. Point to her belly and explain that she has a baby growing inside her. The scan on page 10 is a special photograph that shows a baby inside a mummy's body. The mummy and daddy on page 11 are feeding their hungry babies. The mummy is feeding the baby with milk from her breasts (feel free to use whatever word is most familiar to your child). Parents also feed their babies milk in bottles.

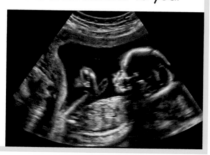

Pages 24-25: Talk about the people your child meets regularly outside of his or her family. Examples might include family friends, the doctor, a dentist, a hairdresser or a friendly assistant in a local shop.

Pages 28-29: Use the photos to discuss feelings and behaviour. For example:
- Why do you think the little boy is sad? (Perhaps the man is his daddy or big brother who has to go away to work.)
- Why is the family excited?
- The brothers are fighting over the scooter. How will they feel after the fight?

Pages 18-19: Ask your child to discuss what is happening in the photos. (The girls on page 18 live in a tiny village in Vietnam. They are collecting wood to burn on fires that their families use for heat and cooking.) Ask your child how he or she helps around the home. For example, does your child help with baking or other kinds of cooking? Does your child tidy away his or her toys before going to bed?

My Family Activities

Make a Family Portrait

Ask your child to draw or paint the people in their family. Sit with your child while they create their picture. Discuss the picture and ask questions – for example, what colour hair does your sister have? What is your pet's name?
To extend this activity, ask your child to draw or paint their home around or alongside the family members. He or she may also wish to add members of their extended family, such as grandparents, cousins or friends.

Create a Handprint Family Tree

Help your child to draw or paint a tree trunk and branches. Make handprints for every member of your child's family, using a different colour for each person. The prints can be made directly onto the tree. Alternatively, the prints can be made onto individual pieces of paper. Then help your child cut out the handprints and glue them to the tree.

Make a Shapes House

Cut different shapes (for example, squares, circles, triangles and rectangles) from coloured paper.
Ask your child to make a picture of their home by sticking the different shapes to a piece of paper.
When the picture is completed, ask your child what each of the different shapes represents – for example, are the squares windows or doors?
What part of the building is shown by the big triangle?

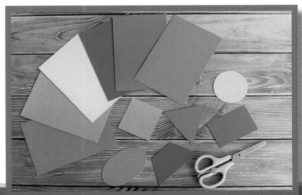